Moses Thursten Runnels

Soil and water pollution:

Presented to the American Public Health Association at New Orleans, Dec.

1880

Moses Thursten Runnels

Soil and water pollution:
Presented to the American Public Health Association at New Orleans, Dec. 1880

ISBN/EAN: 9783337716219

Printed in Europe, USA, Canada, Australia, Japan

Cover: Foto ©ninafisch / pixelio.de

More available books at **www.hansebooks.com**

SOIL

AND

WATER POLLUTION

PRESENTED TO THE

𝕬merican 𝕻ublic 𝕳ealth 𝕬ssociation,

AT NEW ORLEANS, DEC. 1880.

———

By MOSES T. RUNNELS, M. D.,

INDIANAPOLIS.

———

CHICAGO:
DUNCAN BROTHERS.
1880.

SOIL AND WATER POLLUTION.

There is no subject of greater interest to the people than that of
health and the best means of obtaining it. Plenty of wholesome food,
good air and pure water constitute the first essentials of right living.
Any thing which contaminates these prime requisites admits a factor
into the problem of life which seriously vitiates its result. To what
extent agents of adulteration have injured the human family by disease
and death we do not know, but the usual estimate made by sanitarians
is, that nearly one-half of the existing diseases might be abolished, provided that individuals and communities should enter upon correct
modes of living. In the United States over one hundred thousand
persons die annually, and probably one hundred and fifty thousand
persons are constantly sick from causes well known to be preventable. 'Dr. Draper says the total number of deaths in Massachusetts
during five years, 1869–73, from all causes was 156,289 ; of that number the deaths from zymotic or fermentable diseases comprised 26 per
cent.; those from acute pulmonary diseases were 7 per cent.; and
those from phthisis, 17 per cent. So that, if we include all these
among the " preventable" diseases, the deaths from these causes rep-
resent one-half the actual mortality. It is estimated that the produc-
tive efficiency of the average life in this country might be increased
30 per cent.; or up to the normal amount by the proper observance of
health laws. The annual mortality rate should not exceed 15 per 1,000
in cities under good sanitary management, but the tables of the
National Board of Health show a greater mortality in almost every
city of the country. Zymotic or preventable diseases are increasing
in Indianapolis. From these diseases 443 deaths occurred in the city
during the year 1879—over 32 per cent. more than in 1878— and if
such a large number died, it is fair to calculate that twenty times as
many persons were more or less sick from the same causes. Nearly
33 per cent. of the total deaths of the city last year were due to

zymotic diseases. These facts should awaken the public to thorough search for the causes at work producing such a high mortality.

I believe, and it shall be my endeavor to prove, that the increase of zymotic diseases in the city is due in a great measure to causes easily preventable. Man, it is true, is born to sorrow ; but many of these sorrows are of his own creation, or are due to his neglect of established principles. Having determined upon a thorough investigation, we need only to visit the premises, where typhoid fever, scarlet fever, diphtheria, and diseases of this class prevail, to obtain facts enough to solve the problem. Wherever filth abounds, whether in the air, the ground, or the water, there will be a fruitful soil for the propagation of fermentative diseases. To be convinced of the present and past filthy condition of the city, one should take a walk through any of the alleys at noonday, and inhale the foul odors arising constantly from sewers, cess-pools, privies and decaying animal, vegetable, and excrementitious matters thrown out from kitchens and stables. An examination of the kitchen and back-yard of a house is sufficient to prove one of two things, either that Biddy is " monarch of all she surveys," or that the family need a few practical lessons on sanitary science. The latter are sure to follow in time.

The increase of zymotic diseases in Indianapolis, is due largely to soil and water pollution. The conditions of the soil affect our health through the water we drink and the air we breathe. To effluvia from the soil, may be attributed, as stated by Parkes, paroxysmal fevers, typhoid fever, yellow fever, bilious remittent fever, cholera and dysentery. Waring accepts the theory of the dissemination of typhoid fever by fecal discharges of the sick, but gives as his opinion that the disease may be developed by exhalations of decomposing matters in dung-heaps, pig sties, privy vaults, cellars, cess-pools, drains and sewers, or it may be due to the presence of the poison deep in the ground, and its escape in an active condition in ground exhalations. A cold soil, and a misty, chilly condition of the atmosphere are caused by large amounts of water in the ground ; and persons living on such soil are disposed to catarrhal complaints, rheumatism and neuralgia. Dampness of the soil produces malaria and consumption, and their activity varies with the degree of moisture. The lowering of the ground-water in the malarious districts of Indiana, has greatly mitigated the paroxysmal fevers which were formerly so prevalent, and the general healthfulness of the state has been increased by drainage. The sandy soil underlying Indianapolis retains from 33 to 36 per cent. of water. A strong clay soil will not retain over 27 per cent. of water.

Acccording to Pettenkofer, Ford and others, an excessive amount of water in the soil is injurious to health by the effects of dampness. It favors the decomposition of organic matter in the soil, and the evolution of unhealthy effluvia. The water is liable to become polluted, especially when it is the source of supply of water in wells used for drinking purposes. The soil is so damp in Indianapolis, that houses built close to the ground are known to be very unhealthy. At least four-fifths of all the houses in the city are too near the ground, to insure perfect immunity from dampness, and its blasting influences to health.

In the construction of dwellings, care should be taken to provide the most efficient means for excluding dampness from the foundation walls and basement floors ; and the soil should be rendered drier by underground drainage. Fox says, it is very unwise to allow the soil close to houses to be defiled by filth ; for the fires of a house creating a force of suction, draw into the house the air contained in the surrounding soil, as well as of that on which it is built. The popular impression, that the atmosphere ends where the ground begins, is a very widely spread delusion. Most soils are more or less porous. A house built on gravelly soil stands on a foundation composed of a mixture of two parts of small stones and one part of air. The air may give place to any gas or to water. Zymotic diseases have been known to arise from the emanations of soil polluted by excreta, and impurities from sewers and drains and all other filth. Poisoning by breathing the gases generated in sewers and cess-pools is not uncommon. In reference to this point, Dr. Jno. Simon says : " The ferments so far as we know them, show no power of active diffusion in dry air; but as moisture is their normal medium, currents of humid air (as from sewers and drains) can lift them in their full effectiveness, and if into houses or confined exterior spaces, then with their chief chances of remaining effective ; and ill-ventilated, low-lying localities, if unclean as regards the removal of their refuse, may especially be expected to have these ferments present in their common atmosphere as well as of course teeming in their soil and ground water."

Indianapolis **s** in the bottom of a basin, the rim of which rises sixty or seventy feet all round it, east of White river; in some places as at Crown Hill to three times that height.

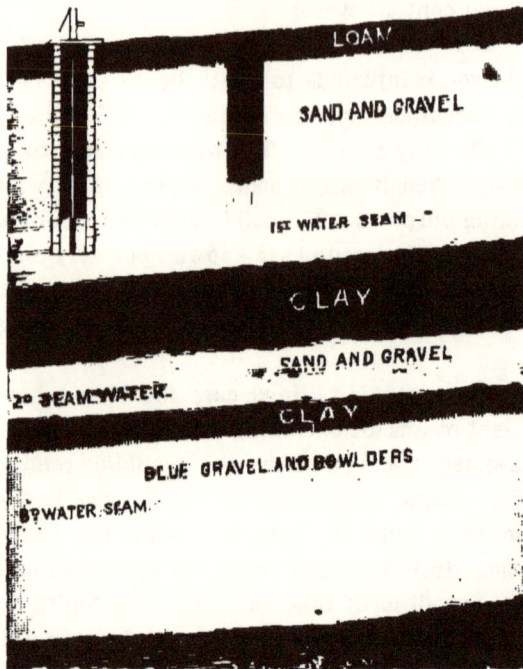

Let us now inquire into the condition of the soil of the city. We find that the general direction of the water trend is from northeast to southwest; that the water level in the wells near the Atlas works is thirty-five feet above the river level at the city water works; and that the waterfall is from fifteen to eighteen feet per mile. The formation of the ground beneath the city is attributed by geologists to the glacial drift of pre-historic times. From seventy to ninety feet below the surface the earth is built up of alternate beds of sand gravel, and clay, and go to show that at some remote period running water with its leveling and transforming power, aided by the corroding force of the air, contributed largely to the geological formation which we find to-day.

After obtaining the distances through these various strata in the different parts of the city, an average is calculated in the following order:

Loam, three to four feet; sand and gravel, thirty to forty feet;

blue compact clay (hard pan), twelve to eighteen feet; sand and gravel, five to ten feet; soft clay, one to five feet; and blue gravel and boulders to Devonian limestone, thirty-five to fifty feet. The first stratum of clay is very hard and tough, and for that reason is called "hard-pan." It has an inclination from the northeast to the southwest of about thirty feet to the mile. The further north and east of White river, the less distance it is to bed rock. Occasionally below the "hard-pan" is found a small drift of soft clay, but this is not usual and does not extend very far in area : often in moving ten feet it is missed. The first seam of water is usually reached at a depth of seventeen to twenty-five feet; the second seam at fifty to sixty-five feet; and the third seam at seventy to ninety feet.

These various strata of water are all what is called "hard water." Prof. E. T. Cox states that "the first seam contains the largest amount of mineral water, principally calcium carbonate, magnesium carbonate, chlorides and ferrous sulphate. The amount of chlorine is so large, that its presence is due in a great measure to sewage contaminations. The second seam of water contains but little chlorides, but has about the same amount of calcic and magnesic carbonates as the first. It is a good potable water when properly protected from contaminations from the upper seam. The third seam of water is also a hard water, that is, its salts will decompose a portion of soap and form a curd ; but it contains less carbonates and more sulphates of the alkaline earths, lime and magnesia." Inasmuch as the object of this paper, is to show to what extent the soil and water of Indianapolis are affected by pollution and the influence such pollution has on health, it is proper to state as nearly as possible, the sources from which the contamination arises. By the assistance of the former civil engineer of the city, the following estimate was made :

Area of Indianapolis (not including ground unimproved) 5,000 acres.

Within the city limits there are :

Surface dug wells..15,000
Driven wells...... ... .,...........................5,000
Open privy vaults...22,000
Privy vaults filled up.. 13,000
Cess-pools.. 10,000
Cess-pools filled up............................... 5,000

The builders of the city state, that in the business portion of the city, it is not uncommon to discover from three to a half dozen old privy vaults, in making a single excavation for an ordinary building.

According to the above estimate which is considered very low, 50,000 privy vaults and cess-pools are constantly filling the soil with deadly poisons, and polluting the water of at least 15,000 surface-dug wells, which furnish drinking water to 50,000 people.

Not more than 6,000 persons drink water from the city water-works, and about 20,000 persons use water from driven wells and cisterns. It is a rule well established by eastern boards of health, that a dug well drains a circular area with a radius equal to twice the distance of the depth of the well. It has been ascertained, that a very large number of the wells of the city are situated within an average distance of less than thirty feet of cess-pools and privy vaults, while a great many are distant from them not over ten feet. Most wells are dug simply with the view of obtaining water and of having it as convenient to hand as possible ; the cess-pools are dug similarly, with a view to convenience except that the demand here is that the liquid contents shall readily drain away. Provided the well furnishes an abundance of water, and the cess-pool allows the liquid refuse to soak away, and on this account, seldom requires cleaning out, there is little concern as to what goes on unobserved beneath the surface of the ground. In the course of time the wellwater is discovered to be impure, after sickness, and perhaps death, have followed its use.

Wells situated on street corners in close proximity to the catch basin of the sewers, are extremely liable to pollution from leakage from the foul gutters and seepage from the catch basins.

A notable outbreak of typhoid fever occurred in Louisville, in the autumn of 1875, from the use of wellwater contaminated by a privy in an adjoining school yard. The water was found to be impure, and the well was condemned. "In the summer of 1878 some forty persons in Rochester whose supply of drinking water was derived from a certain well, were taken sick with typhoid fever and other zymotic diseases." The health officers closed the well and the people got water from other sources. They began to recover immediately.

"All authorities agree that any well situated within a few feet of a cess-pool or sewer should be regarded with grave suspicion, for the intervening soil may become overdone with filth at any moment, and cease to act as an efficient filter of the polluted water, and allow organic matter to enter the well ; or animal filth may be washed into the well at any time by a hard rain."

A great many citizens of Indianapolis are drinking water exclusively from cisterns. It is difficult to estimate the number of cisterns within the city limits; but a great deal may be said in regard to the general unwholesomeness of the water they contain. Rain water contains a small proportion of chlorine, the amount varying with the condition of the atmosphere, and the purity of the shedding surface.

When pure rain falls upon a roof it carries down with it all the impurities accumulated there during dry weather; these soon putrify in the cistern, and infect the water.

The majority of the cisterns in the city are faulty in some particular—either proper care was not exercised in their construction, or the necessary repairs were not made in due time—and they are found to be seeping, or leaky. Sufficient attention is not given to keeping the cisterns well closed, and the result is that filth in large quantities is to be found on emptying them. During my examinations I have met with many cistern waters in the city so polluted by sewage infiltration, that an immediate interdict on their use appeared to be called for. Owing to the impurity of the soil, sewage matter finds its way into hundreds of cisterns, and contaminates the water. Many of our cisterns contain water rank with vegetable or animal impurity, and the contents of the greater portion of these are not above suspicion. Some of them are neither more or less than shallow wells, receiving more of their contents by percolation than by inflow above.

Last December 458 cisterns in Memphis, Tenn., were examined with the following result: Sound, 209; seeping, eighty-two; and undoubtedly leaking, 167. In the total number, there were 249 condemned as unfit for use. To what extent these leaky cisterns contributed to the epidemic of yellow fever we cannot tell. The probability of sewage contamination in each instance was strong.

In the year of 1879 there were seventy-eight deaths from typhoid and typho-malarial fevers in Indianapolis. It may be stated as a probable fact, that our siege of fevers in 1879 originated and was afterward propagated in polluted drinking water, and ill-ventilated apartments poisoned by sewer gases, or in close proximity to foul and overflowing water closets and cess-pools. Forty-three per cent. of the total deaths in the city in 1879 were deaths of children under five years of age. Among the general causes of the high death rate of infants, may be mentioned poverty and ignorance. These two conditions existing in the parents, are great enemies of the public health and are two important factors which go to make up this startling infantile mortality. But it must be conceded that typhoid fever, scarlet fever, diphtheria, measles, hooping cough and diarrhœal diseases have been endemic in our midst as the result of foul air and polluted water. Deaths from these causes occur more or less at all ages, but distinctively more among children. The influence of filth causes the infants and young children- to die at twice, or thrice, or four times their fair standard rate of mortality ; and this disproportion seems to mark the young lives as finer tests of soil and water pollution than are the acclimated adults. The board of health of Indianapolis report that hundreds of cellars in this city are full, or partly full of water, the entire year ; and that the increase of zymotic diseases is due largely to wet and damp cellars, as well as to the long continued and general practice of covering up foul privy vaults, after they have become full, to save the expense of removing the contents.

Being thoroughly impressed with the facts above enumerated, I commenced to make investigations. I employed a competent chemist, Mr. Jno. Hurty, to make sanitary examinations of water, and assist me in the work.

In the collection of samples of water, special care was exercised in regard to cleanliness and to avoid introducing any errors into our examinations. Below I give a tabular statement of the analyses of waters taken from surface dug wells in the city. Excepting the permanganate of potash test, the quantities are in one litre (22-100ths of an imperial gallon).

	TOTAL SOLIDS.	MATTER, ORGANIC & VOL- ATILE.	CHLOR- INE.	PER MANGA- NATE TEST.	ALBUMI- NOID AMMO- NIA.	FREE AMMO- NIA.	REMARKS.
	Gramme.	Gramme.	Gramme.	Drops.	Gramme.	Gramme.	
Sample 1.	0.81	.09	.11	30	.0524	not obt'd	Very bad.
„ 2.	1.061	.179	.06	24	.00015	.00009	Suspicious.
„ 3.	1.26	.20	.115	38	not obt'd	not obt'd	Very bad.
„ 4.	0.94	.131	.093	22	not obt'd	not obt'd	Bad.
„ 5.	0.80	.055	.032	11	.00009	.00001	Suspicious.
„ 6.	0.964	.098	.08	15	.00011	.0 001	Suspicious.
„ 7.	0.798	.178	.104	28	.00089	.00005	Very bad.
„ 8.	.37	.025	.049	12	.0003	.0004	Suspicious,

In regard to the wholesomeness or unwholesomeness of water, Watt's Dictionary of Chemistry gives the following : " Water suitable for economical, technical or culinary purposes should not contain of solid constituents to exceed five-tenths of a gramme to one gramme per litre. Water containing one-tenth gramme per litre of organic matter is unfit for culinary purposes or drinking. Wholesome water should not contain of organic matter more than five-one thousanth to one one-hundredth gramme per liter. As a rule, water containing as much as one one-hundredth of a gramme of chlorine per litre may be suspected of being contaminated with drainage. Whenever in water the oxygen amounts to less than one-third of the nitrogen, and the water also causes a considerable reduction of permanganate of potash, the presence of decomposing organic substance is probable. The capability of water to remain for some days at a temperature of about 22° C, without undergoing decomposition is of great importance in reference to the question of wholesomeness."

The permanganate of potash test given above was as follows : The test solution was distilled water, one litre, and permanganate of potash, one gramme. Of this solution, the number of drops required to render fifty cubic centimetres of the water under examination permanently red, were reported. It should be understood that the same quantity of distilled water required but eight drops of the test solution to become permanently red.

The first sample of water was taken from a well where fourteen persons were simultaneously attacked in December last by typho-malarial and diarrhœal diseases. All had been drinking water from this well, and had it not been for the timely help of the physician who condemned the water,

SERIOUS RESULTS WOULD HAVE FOLLOWED.

On examination the cess-pool was found to be connected directly with the well by a pipe, and when the cess-pool became full, its contents regurgitated into the well. The Board of Health examined the premises, condemned the well and ordered that both privy vault and cess-pool be cleaned out without delay. I understand that it is quite common in this city to connect the cess-pool with the well by a pipe so that the waste water may be readily conveyed away ; but if people knew the danger to be feared from such an arrangement, greater care in the construction of drains would be exercised. Hundreds of cases might be related where in houses fitted with all that taste could desire, and gold procure, a siphoned trap, or in the absence of a trap, an imperfect joint, or an old brick drain, or riddled soil pipe, defects easily remedied if known to exist, have undermined the health of adults and slain the little ones. In the first sample a large quantity of animalculæ were revealed by the microscope. Fox states that " the existence of animal life in a water affords good evidence in itself of the presence of a very sensible amount of organic matter, *alias* filth. These little creatures feed and flourish on what we call organic matter, and in perfectly pure water they cannot live. A perfectly pure water contains no suspended matter nor any animal or vegetable life. The ova of the round and the thread worms, the eggs and joints of the tapeworm and small leeches, which may give rise to grave disorders, should not be forgotten in making microscopic examinations of drinking waters."

Good water is both a necessity and a priceless blessing. Foul water is a scourge and a messenger of death. No one except a brute would hesitate which to choose if he could tell one from the other. It is only with the grosser pollution of water that chemists can apply their science. Infinitesimal pollution cannot be estimated by the skill of any chemist. It is the careful physician who decides more accurately in regard to the purity of water than the chemist. Sir. Benj. Brodie in speaking of the detection of infinitesimal pollution says: "I think you have a much better chance of getting at these relations through accurate medical statistics, properly applied, than you have through chemical analysis, because chemical analysis is one of the poorest things possible to reach those delicate quantities. You cannot get at these small quantities at all; chemical analysis must be limited by our power of weighing and measuring. It may go on to a certain point, but we cannot go beyond that point."

The well from which the second sample was taken, was within twenty-five feet of a privy vault twenty feet deep. Several families used water from the well. Two cases of

TYPHOID FEVER DEVELOPED

in one family, and all the persons who drank the water were constantly ailing. The third sample was taken from a well where four cases of typhoid fever had occurred. A thorough search had been made for the cause of the trouble. The well water had been suspected and was condemned by the attending physician.

Seventy feet from the wall there was a privy vault overflowing. Another vault was within twenty-five feet of the well. To the effluvia from the former was attributed one case of typhoid fever. The stench was so great at night that not even the windows in the upper stories of the houses in the neighborhood could be kept open. People living near had sore throats, malarial fever and diarrhœal disorders.

The fourth sample was obtained from a surface-dug well, from which the inmates of the State Female Reformatory were supplied with drinking water. Since the first of last August thirty-nine cases of well defined typhoid fever, and thirteen milder cases of the same disease appeared in the Reformatory. The attending physician attributed the outbreak of the fever to the water from the well. After a thorough chemical examination of the water, the well was condemned and filled up, and the water supply now comes from a driven well.

It is worthy of remark that the persons attacked by typhoid fever, had been daily drinking the foul water from the well until the appearance of the fever; that the immediate surroundings of the well and the sanitary condition of the building were good, and that no direct cause of typhoid fever outside of the well could be discovered.

The fifth sample was taken from a well which supplied a family of six persons with water. Diarrhœal troubles.

SYMPTOMS OF TYPHOID FEVER,

sore throats, etc., were not uncommon, and the family physician was frequently consulted. One privy vault forty feet north from the well was full. Another privy vault was fifty feet northeast of the well. The contents of the vaults undoubtedly contaminated the well water to some extent, and of course the evil would be increased with time.

The sixth sample was drawn from a well on the south side of the city. No privy vault or cess-pool is located within fifty feet of it. To all appearances the surroundings are good. The well water has been used for drinking purposes for several years. One person in the family had typhoid fever three years ago, and malarial and bilious attacks have annoyed the other members of the family frequently.

The seventh sample was obtained from a well from which three cases of typhoid fever had previously been supplied with water. The attending physician attributed the development of the disease to the unwholesomeness of the water.

The eighth sample was obtained from one of the wells at the water works.

The following table gives the analyses of waters from *driven wells* extended below the first or second stratum of clay. These wells are located in different parts of the city. Excepting the permanganate of potash test, previously explained, the quantities are in one litre.

	TOTAL SOLIDS.	MATTER ORGANIC & VOL-ATILE.	CHLOR-INE.	PER MANGA-NATE TEST.	ALBU-MINOID AMMO-NIA.	FREE AMMO-NIA.	REMARKS.
	Grammes	Grammes	Grammes	Drops.	Grammes	Grammes	
Sample 1.	0.400	.012	.008	10	.00045	none	Good water.
„ 2.	0.586	.28	.004	12	.00005	none	Good water.
„ 3.	0.690	.047	.025	9	none	none	Excellent.
„ 4.	0.496	.08	.006	10	none	none	Excellent.
„ 5.	0.454	.069	.038	9	one	.0001	Excellent.

I have in my possession partial and complete analyses by Prof. E. T. Cox, of waters from nine other driven wells in the city. The analyses show that these wells furnish good potable water.

The occupants of large buildings are often supplied with water from tanks on the upper floors. If the tanks are not properly constructed and well inclosed, the water pumped into them may be contaminated at any time by impurities.

Given below are analyses of waters drawn from tanks in large blocks.

The quantities are in one litre

	TOTAL SOLIDS.	MATTER ORGANIC & VOL-ATILE.	CHLOR-INE.	FREE AMMO-NIA.	ALBU-MINOID AMMO-NIA	REMARKS.
	Grammes	Grammes	Grammes	Grammes	Grammes	
Sample 1.	1.02	.14	.09	.00004	.00012	.... Bad.
„ 2.	.554	.089	.075	.00015	.00009	............Good.

One person who lived in the former block died of typhoid fever, and many others had sickness from the use of the water.

The question of drainage and water supply of cities, should take the precedence of every other question, for upon its proper solution depends thousands of lives. Those in authority should understand its importance, and feel the pressing necessity of more thorough sanitary work. Hygiene is not only a subject of scientific interest to the medical man, but its problems and discoveries ought to be of great practical importance to political economists and legislators, who usually occupy themselves with subjects which benefit the common people very little. It appears that the best engineering talent, and great amounts of money, have been employed, to furnish cities and towns with *inexhaustible supplies of water without sufficient regard to quality.*

To economically furnish water in ample quantity, is an object of great importance; but it is of more consequence that the water obtained is not contaminated by sewers, cess-pools, and surface drainage to such an extent that disease and death shall be scattered broadcast; among those who drink the water. There are those who claim that a small proportion of sewage in drinking water does not necessarily prove deleterious to health.

The English Rivers' Pollution Commission published conclusions based on the examination of some two thousand samples of water claimed to be drinkable; condemning river water because it is liable to contamination from drainage of cultivated land, towns and manufactories. According to their decision "the admixture of even a small quantity of the infected discharges (of persons suffering from cholera or typhoid fever), with a large volume of drinking water, is sufficient for the propagation of those diseases among persons using such water."

Dr. Folsom, in the report of the Massachusetts State Board of Health, states that "excessive dilution simply diminishes the chances of danger from any particular tumblerful." To show how disease may be transmitted in dilute sewage and that disease germs are not exterminated by diffusion through a large body of running water, Dr. E. D. Mapother, of Dublin, reports forty cases of typhoid fever occuring in a hospital which received its supply from a river. The cause was traced to some barracks twenty-five miles higher up, from which typhoidal dejections had been emptied through drains into the river.

The following classification of drinkable waters which was made by the English commissioners, should be received by us as entirely trustworthy.

Wholesome — Spring water, deep well water, and upland surface water.

Suspicious—Stored rain water, and surface water from cultivated land.

Dangerous—River water to which sewage gets access, and shallow well water.

The fact that foul water will breed disease, should no longer be ignored. The citizens of Indianapolis have been drinking water from the city water works not above suspicion, and it is about time that the pollution of the water by filth should excite public attention.

Below I give analyses of samples of water drawn at different times and places from the faucets of the city water works.

The following report is from Prof. Thos. C. Van Nuys, of the State University.

BLOOMINGTON, Ind., May 10, 1880.

The water you sent on Thursday was received on Friday evening. The following is the report of my chemical and microscopic examinations:

In one litre (1,000 cubic centimetres).

Nitric acid anhydride, N2, O5.	10.72	milligrammes
Ammonia, NH3,	0.03	"
Carbonic acid anhydride, CO2.	0.439	gramme.
Calcium oxide, Ca, O,	0.148	"
Magnesium oxide, Mg, O,	0.04128	"
Chlorine,	0.09218	"
Degree of hardness (English)	25.7	

The organic matter in 100 cubic centimetres of the water required 3.11 cubic centimetres of the 1-100 normal solution of potassium permanganate to oxidize it; therefore one litre of the water would require 31.1 cubic centimetres of the 1-100 normal solution K Mn O4 to oxidize the organic matter. In 31.1 c. c. of this solution there is 0.0098 gramme K Mn O4 or 0.0247 gramme oxygen liberated. I would remark here that there is no method of estimating the exact quantity of organic matter in water. The method of estimating the carbon and hydrogen by combustion analysis (Frankland and Armstrong's) has been found defective,—also the methods based on the estimation of nitrogen and reduction of silver oxide. The method employed in this case (Schultze's) is the most reliable, and yet not all the organic matter is oxidized, for some is volatized in boiling.

I found the following infusorial animalaculæ: Stylonchia pustulata, actinurus neptunius, rotirfer vulgaris, monostylaquadridentata, navicular baltica.

I give here the magnified pictures.

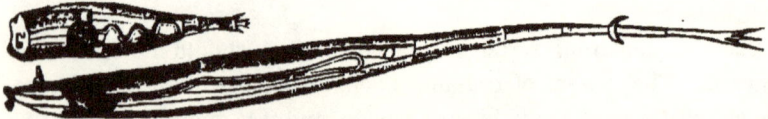

Actinurus Neptunius.

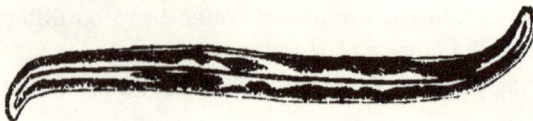

Navicula Baltica.

Monosty in Quadridentata.

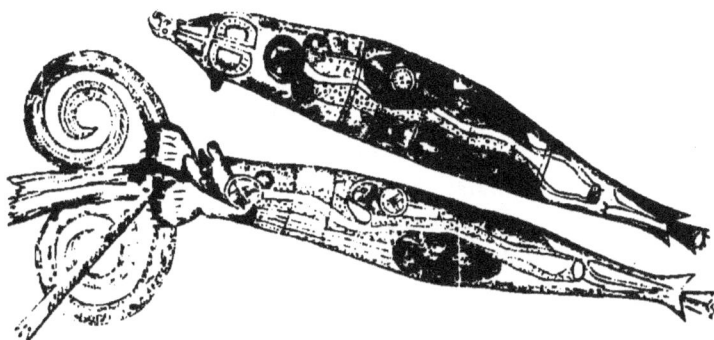

Rotifer Vulgaris.

Stylonchia Pustulata.

I did not examine the first sample of water with the microscope. In the water of the second bottle I found but one kind of infusoria, *viz.*, stylonchia pustulata, but they were numerous. In the water sent on Thursday I found the others named, but few in number. In both samples of water there was but a small quantity of mineral matter, a few crystals of Ca CO3. The water was somewhat cloudy and the suspended particles were evidently of vegetable origin. I have not adopted any standard in judging water for drinking purposes.

As yet none has been found having a scientific basis. But let us see how this water would be rated by some of the standards of men who have justly distinguished themselves by their labor in water analysis.

The Grenzzahlen limitary numbers are of E. Reichardt, Kubel, and Tiemann and Fischer.

One litre (1,000 cubic centimetres).

	REICHARDT.	KUBEL AND TIE-MANN.	FISCHER.
Nitric acid anhyd...	4 milligrammes.	5 to 15 milligramm.	27 milligrammes.
Chlorine...............	24 ,,	20 to 30 ,,	35 ,,
Lime (Ca. O.:			112 ,,
Magnesia (Mg. O.)...			40 ,,
Degrees of hardness			
(German)	18 ,,	18 to 20 ,,	17 ,,

This water contains in milligrammes per litre: Nitric Acid Anhyd. 10.72; Chlorine, 92.18; Lime, 14.8 ; Magnesia, 41 ; degrees of hardness (German), 20.596.

The limitary quantity of organic matter in 100 c. c. should not exceed that necessary for the deoxidation of K Mn O4 in 2 c. c. of the 1-100 normal solution. This is given by Fresenius. For 100 c. c. of this water 3.11 c. c. of the 1-100 normal solution was required. The organic matter in the water is considerable, yet is no doubt variable in quantity. On account of the quantity of the organic matter, by exposure to the air doubtless many other species of infusoria would be formed. The water is hard and by chemical technologists would be condemned, as with them 10 degrees German, or 12.5 degrees English, is the limit.

The ammonia is in a mere trace, yet accurately estimated as given. Nearly all rain water contains more. I have estimated the chlorine in water sent on Thursday last (by the volumetric method), and found 0.05902 gramme chlorine in one litre. This makes a difference of 0.0322 gramme chlorine as found in one litre of the water of the first bottle sent. In what way could there be such a great increase or rather decrease of the chlorides ? Are there any privy vaults or slaughter houses near the source of the water ? May I ask where this water was obtained ?

In a letter of March 12, 1880, Prof. E. T. Cox gives the following : " I fully believe that whenever any form of disease rages as an epidemic in any locality, it is due in a large measure to water pollution The three streams of subterranean water beneath Indianapolis, flow from northeast to southwest. Wells that are supplied from the upper water, contain more and more chloride of sodium (common salt) as you go to the south part of the city, and this is absolute proof of sewer-pollution, and all the well water from the first and second seams is absolutely dangerous, and its use should be prohibited. The lower stratum is safe if the upper seams are shut off from it. When water works were first contemplated at Indianapolis, I was called upon for information, and had my advise been taken, you would now have the best possible water, instead of water of doubtful character, to use the mildest term." On the 20th of March a sample of water was obtained from the water works for examination. The analysis showed in one litre,

Total solids, ...985	gramme
Organic and volatile, ...08	"
Chlorine, . . . , ...055	"

Fifty centimetres of the water required fourteen drops of the permanganate of potash solution to render it permanently red. The same amount of distilled water required but eight drops. The microscope, with a lens of 100 diameters, revealed considerable vegetable matter.

Inasmuch as White river is used by the water works as a source of supply when the water in their wells get low, and also in time of fire in the city, it was thought advisable to ascertain the condition of the river water. Therefore, on April 30, 1880, a sample was drawn from the river at middle of the iron bridge at the foot of Washington street.

One litre contained:

Total solid constituents......................	.36 gramme.
Organic and volatile matter.................	.032	"
Chlorine	.105	"
Free ammonia...............................	.00072	"
Albuminoid ammonia.......................	.00048	"

Fifty cubic centimetres of this water required thirty-six drops of the permanganate of potash solution to render it permanently red. The same amount of distilled water required but eight drops of said solution to become permanently red.

The microscope revealed sand, clay, legs. and other parts of insects, foreign matter of many kinds, and animalculæ. This water is but little better than sewage. It is due to the water works to state that the water taken from the river is filtered through a bed of sand and gravel about four feet deep.

Professor Edward R. Taylor, of Cleveland, examined two samples of water from the water-works with the following result:

	1st sample.	2d sample.
Specific gravity...10010	10021
In grains per litre the analyses show		
Solid residue... .5876	.5696

Organic and volatile matter	.3150	.1213
Chlorine	.0598	.0738
Free ammonia	.0015	.0002
Albuminoid ammonia	.0038	.0018

The amount of chlorine is very considerable in both samples. It would properly be presumed that both had a bad origin.

The following is taken from *The State Press*, Iowa City, Iowa, April 14, 1880 :

" The Des Moines City Council spent several days inspecting the various systems of water works through Iowa, Illinois and Indiana and came back discouraged and disgusted with what they had seen." The *Leader* says : " The last report made was from Indianapolis, where the water was bad, the contract bad, and all the conditions were very bad. But for that matter those things are getting monotonous. On the whole route, from Burlington to Peoria, water was not found fit to drink, and in several places it was too bad to wash in. At Springfield water is taken out of the Illinois river, thick and black, and pumped about the city without even an excuse made toward filtering it, and yet the money spent on her water works aggregates nearly three times the hundred thousand of dollars the works in Des Moines are offered at. The State Board of Health has declared the water unfit for use. At Indianapolis the Secretary of the Water Company said they could not recommend the water ; at Burlington, with her new and cheap works, the filter is reported broken and the yellow Mississippi mud is daily dished up for men to wash their eyes in. There was no excuse made for the mixture of mud and water at Keokuk, it is probably past the day of excuses."

On May 18, 1880, a sample of water was drawn from a faucet of the Water Works Company. The analysis revealed the following. Each litre contained :

Total solids	.84 gramme.
Organic and volatile matter	.43 "
Chlorine	.047 "
Free ammonia	.0000S "
Albuminoid ammonia	.00024 "
Nitrates and nitrites	Large amount.

The value of the above figures can best be understood when it is known that pure spring water never contains over .000005 gramme of free ammonia, and .00002 gramme albuminoid ammonia per litre. The best authorities state that, that water is suspicious which contains above .0001 gramme of albuminoid ammonia per litre ; and over

.00015 gramme of albuminoid ammonia per litre ought to condemn absolutely.

Another sample of water from the water works was sent to Prof. Van Nuys, on May 27, 1880. He reports that the water contained much more organic matter than that in which an estimation of organic matter was made before.

The following statement is from Prof. Van Nuys, July 14, 1880, in regard to water from the water works. *Chemical and microscopic examination of water received from Dr. M. T. Runnels, of Indianapolis,* on *June* 23 *and* 29, 1880:

"The organic matter in 100 cubic centimetres of the water required 5.35 cubic centimetres of the one one-hundredth normal potassium permanganate solution. In 5.35 cubic centimetres of this solution there are 1.6932 milligrammes potassium permanganate or 0.423 milligramme oxygen was liberated, hence in one litre of the water the organic matter would require 53.5 cubic centimetres of the one one-hundredth normal permanganate solution, or 4.23 milligrammes oxygen would combine with the carbon and hydrogen of the organic matter.

Residue (one litre filtered) heated to 180° centimetres......... 473 8
Chlorine.. 189.3
Nitric acid anhyd ($N^2 O^5$)................................... 17.448
Nitrous acid anhyd ($N^2 O^3$)................................. a trace
Ammonia ($N H^3$)... 0.38
Calcium oxide ($Ca O$).. 128.8
Magnesium oxide ($Mg O$)...................................... 46.2
Degree of hardness, English................................... 21.93
    or, degree of hardness, German............................ 17.54

No microscopic examination was made of the water received June 23d. In that received June 29th, there were numerous flakes of what appeared to be organic bodies with granular matter, the following infusorial animalculæ were found:

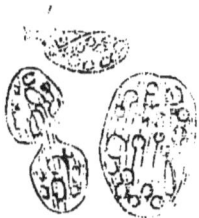

Closterium Acerosum.

Glaucoma scintillans.

a Monas crepusculum.
b Monas punctum.

The residue, organic matter, chlorine, nitric acid anhyd, and ammonia were estimated in the water received June 23d. The calcium and magnesium were estimated in the water received June 29, 1880."

Although much has lately been said regarding impure water and the startling mortality of Indianapolis, there are a great many people who persistently refuse to accept the facts and would rather submit to a large death rate than to "clean up" or go to the necessary expense of obtaining good water. The complaint is often made that doctors do not discharge their duties in warning the people against the dangers of sickness. The fact is that the medical profession gives enough wholesome advice to the public, but very few persons make practical use of the information kindly given.

I commenced last January a series of soil and water investigations. A partial report of my investigations was published in the Indianapolis *News*, May 25 and July 13, 1880, and the Indianapolis *Saturday Herald*, June 5, 1880. Since that time with the assistance of the best chemists I have zealously prosecuted the work.

It is not an exaggeration to say that no dug well within a mile of Circle street, can be depended upon for a continuous supply of good water. The water furnished to the people by the water works company is no better than the water from the average dug well. Water from deep driven wells is the best well water we have.

I found the alleys, by-ways, back-yards and stables all through the city in a very filthy condition. Privy vaults have been dug without being cemented, and no care whatever has been taken to keep them clean.

The drainage of the city is very defective. It is only along a few of the principal streets that sewers have been constructed, and the greater portion of the city has no drainage at all. It is a very common thing to find standing water and large mud holes in every direction through the city. It is a notable fact that the water level in many cellars corresponds with the water level of dug wells and privy vaults adjacent. Is it any wonder that infant mortality is so great in the city ?

If "infants of one year and under drink but little water," they do breathe in this city the deadly gases developed by the action of the hot sun on decaying organic and vegetable matters, and the effluvia arising constantly from overflowing privy vaults and cess-pools.

Sickness is sure to follow and death may abruptly terminate the young life. According to the report of the Board of Health the deaths in this city have been since January 1, 1876, as follows :

```
In 1876 the number of deaths were..................... 1,641
"  1877  "       "     "     "     "     ............... ...... 1,528
"  1878  "       "     "     "     "     ................... 1,296
"  1879  "       "     "     "     "     ..................... 1,470
"  1880  "       "     "     "     "     (9 months............ 1,352
```
                                                      ———
```
        Total.............................. .................. 7,287
```

Assuming that the population has been 75,125, the annual death rate would be :

```
21.8 per 1,000 in....... ............................... 1876
20.3  "      "    "  ......................................... .... 1877
17.2  "      "    "  ......................................... 1878
19.5  "      "    "  ... ...................................... 1879
23.9  "      "    "  (9 months)............................. 1880
```

The average would be 20.5 per 1,000 annually which is at least six above what it should be.

Herewith I give a table of recent sanitary analyses of our city well and cistern waters, which startlingly outline the impending dangers and serve as texts for many cases of ill health and death already met by those who have drank the waters.

The first and second samples were taken from two wells in the rear of a block having about twenty occupants. An inspection of the back yard and alley showed an immense amount of filth. There was no sewer to carry away slop or excrementitious matters. A large privy vault was in the rear of the block. There was one well north and another south of the vault, and about twenty feet from it. These wells supplied the water to the occupants of the block. Six cases of scarlet fever were there developed and three of them died. The other persons in the block were constantly ailing. One of the leading physicians of the city attributed the outbreak of the fever to the bad surroundings and the impure water.

The third sample was taken from a well on East Walnut street. The family using the water were more or less sick all the time. Languor, loss of appetite and spirits, sleeplessness, or nightmare, morning diarrhœa, headache and nausea, one or all, continually annoyed those drinking the water. The privy vault, twelve feet deep was forty feet northeast of the well.

The fourth sample was obtained from a well on North Tennessee street. Throat affections, fevers, diarrhœas, headaches with malaise, etc., made up the list of the complaints of the family using the water.

The fifth sample came from a well on North Alabama street. During the last three months, among those who drank the water there were three who had scarlet fever—one of whom died. And so on similar reports can be made of the other samples, except those marked "good" or "excellent."

SANITARY ANALYSIS OF WELL WATERS.

WHERE FROM	GRAMS PER LITRE.			PARTS PER MILLION.		Nitr'tes and Nitrites	Degree of Hardn.	OPINION.
	Total Solids.	Organ. Volat.	Chlorine.	Free Amm.	Alb. Amm.			
Susqueh. st.	1.53	.02	.117	.12	.33	much	3	Bad.
Susquch. st.	.88	.33	.088	.07	.16	much	2½	Bad.
East Waln. st	1.32	.72	.127	.04	.18	much	1½	Bad.
N. Tenn. st.	.04	.41	.077	.05	.0612	much	2	Suspicious.
N. Alaban. st	1.126	.616	.096	.055	.057	much	3 3-10	Bad.
N. Ills. st.	.60	.18	.043	.01	.'4	much	2½	Very bad.
N. Merid. st.	.24	.012	.008	trace.	trace.	trace.	1½	Excellent.
N. Alabama	.68	.30	.045	.01	.14	little.	2	Suspicious.
Hoyt Av.	.30	.16	.0018	.12	.04	little.	1	Good.
N. Penn. st.	1.41	.03	.075	.24	.4	much	½	Rotten cist.
Blackford st.	.78	.28	.038	.04	.4	much	1½	Very bad.
N.N.Jersey st	.798	.178	.104	.05	.39	much	2	Bad.
E. Ohio st.	1.032	0.5	.09	.04	.19	much	4	Bad.

NAME.	GRAMS PER LITRE.			PARTS pr MILL.		Nitrates and Nitrites	Degree of Hardn.	OPINION.
	Total Solids.	Organ. & Vol.	Chlorine.	Free Amm.	Alb. Amm.			
E. Verm't st	.008	.36	.058	.12	.13	small	6	Very susp.
Davidson st	.848	.34	.08	.20	.08	large	6½	Very susp.
E. St. Joseph	.788	.21	.035	.06	.22	large	4.2	Bad.
E. Mich. st	1.588	.96	.09	.12	.202	large	5½	Bad.
N. Tenn. st	.068	.48	.07	.06	.28	large	3½	Bad.
N. Penu. st	.928	.4	.065	.025	.20	large	5	Bad.
New York st	.5	.13	.04	none	none	none	3½	Excellent.
N. East st	1.788	.874	.09	.08	.22	large	4	Bad.
Irvington	.697	.29	.04	none	.03	small	3½	Good.
N. Merid st	1.06	.57	.10	.08	.164	large	3½	Bad.
N. Delaw. st	.86	.36	.95	.07	.10	large	5	Bad.
N. Tenn. st	.44	.14	.007	.01	.00	none	2	Driven good
Blind Asyl'm	.65	.214	.025	.01	.042	{ heavy slight	2½	Driven good
N. East st	1.00	.62	.34	.114	.142	large	4	Very bad.
322 N. Miss. st	.66	.321	.043	.03	.234	large	4½	Very bad.

NAME.	GRAMS PER LITRE.			PARTS pr MILL.		Nitrates and Nitrites	Degree of Hardn.	OPINION.
	Total Solids.	Organ. & Vol.	Chlorine.	Free Amm.	Alb. Amm.			
Blackford st	0.78	0.39	0.38	.04	.4	large	6½	Bad.
Peru st	0.54	0.36	0.025	.03	.13	small	12	Suspicious.
N. Penn. st.	0.65	0.38	0.03	.08	.10	small	3	Suspicious.
N. Alab. st.	0.48	0.24	0.059	.06	.06	small	7	Good.
N. Delaw. st.	0.54	0.22	0.31	.020	.182	large	4	Bad.
School st.	0.994	0.414	0.10	.04	.16	large	5½	Very bad.
East Ohio st.	1.04	0.63	0.47	.12	.22	large	7	Abominable.
Mass. av.	0.89	0.39	0.213	.07	.13	large	4½	Bad.
E. Ohio	0.802	0.374	0.121	.04	.10	large	3½	Bad.
N. N. Jersey	0.78	0.29	0.08	.03	.13	large	3½	Bad.
E. Pratt	0.60	0.28	0.074	.02	.09	large	4	Bad.
F. Maryland	0.99	0.47	0.111	.07	.199	large	7	Very bad.
Bellfontain	0.49	0.19	0.004	.03	.022	small	4	Good.
Christian av.	0.67	0.23	0.012	.035	.06	large	4	Passably g'd
East Verm't	0.59	0.19	0.12	.03	.09	large	3½	Suspicious.

SANITARY ANALYSIS OF WELL WATERS.

NAME.	GRAMS PER LITRE.			PARTS pr MILL.		Nitrates and Nitrites.	Degree of Hardn.	OPINION.
	Total Solids.	Organ. & Vola.	Chlorine.	Free Amm.	Alb. Amm.			
N. Alab. st	.832	.56	.059	.70	.12	large	4½	Very susp.
N. Alab. st	.79	.39	.055	.64	.10	large	5	Very susp.
N. N. Jersey	.82	.39	.09	.06	.09	med.	5	Susp cious.
N. N. Jersey	.91	.40	.055	.08	.12	large	5	Bad.
Alab. & Waln	.87	.39	.067	.11	.10	large	4½	Bad.
N. Penn. st	1.04	.62	.111	.16	.204	large	7	Very bad.
Oak st	.57	.24	.014	.02	.009	small	4	Good.
E. Verm't st	.66	.29	.04	.05	.07	small	4½	Good.
S. Merid. st	.89	.385	.07	.07	.09	large	6	Very susp.
S. Penn. st	1.24	.81	.22	.19	.22	large	7	Abominable.
S. Penn. st	.87	.33	.072	.095	.088	large	5	Bad.
Vir. Av.	1.12	.59	.79	.11	.29	large	4½	Very bad.
E. Wash. st	.79	.33	.09	.107	.18	large	4½	Bad.
N. West st	.83	.42	.07	.007	.083	large	6½	Bad.
E. South st	.74	.22	.03	.03	.06	med.	5	Passable.

NAME.	GRAMS PER LITRE.			PARTS pr MILL.		Nitrites and Nitrates.	Degree Hardn.	OPINION.
	Total Solids.	Organ. & Vola.	Chlorine.	Free Amm.	Alb. Amm.			
S. East st	.82	.39	.05	.037	.114	large	5	Bad.
E. Market st	.97	.32	.12	.049	.23	v. large	4½	Very bad.
E. Mich. st	1.12	.57	.07	.072	.17	large	4½	Very bad.
Central av.	.607	.22	.044	.041	.09	med.	6½	Suspicious.
Laurel st.	.92	.38	.089	.105	.38	v. large	6½	Very bad.
East Georgia	.62	.49	.072	1.08	.427	large	1½	Very bad.
Broadway st	.63	.30	.022	.03	.04	small	7	Good.
East N. Y. st	.59	.21	.094	.07	.07	large	6½	Bad.
N. N. Jersey	.66	.24	.07	.08	.009	large	7	Bad.
N. N. Jersey	.68	.22	.075	.09	.066	larie	6½	Bad.
N. Illinois st	.80	.31	.03	.039	.113	large	6½	Suspicious.
Hoyt av.	.30	.06	0.1	.04	.06	small	4	Good.
W. St Clair st	.83	.32	0.7	.045	.112	large	7	Very susp.
N. Tenn. st	.69	.27	0.55	.07	.09	med.	6½	Very susp.
N. Tenn. st	.66	.19	.065	.09	.11	large	6½	Very susp.
W. North st	.74	.30	.04	.09	.12	large	6½	Bad.
E. North st	.69	.28	.03	.08	.08	large	6½	Suspicious.
N. Delaw. st	.75	.29	.075	.07	.11	large	7	Bad.

J. N. HURTY, Analyst.

It is very surprising to me that many people are so ignorant in regard to impure water and its deleterious effect on health. I have met with " would be " highly educated persons who have regarded, and do regard any agitation of this subject, as of little value to the public, and as very damaging to the fair fame of the city, and for that reason to be at all hazards covered up and kept secret.

They also express the thought that every kind of water is filled with microscopic creatures, and that a small amount of filth or dirt in drinking water does no special harm. to anyone. All this is the opposite of the facts. Prof. Barnard, of Cornell University, says : " Pure water is not inhabited by organisms; on the contrary stagnant water or impure water alone affords them subsistence. They hasten the destruction of dead animal and vegetable matters the waters may contain, causing for the time being an infusion or fermentation."

Macdonald states that "mineral particles may affect health on account of their mechanical action, as for example when mineral silt or clay causes diarrhœa. Dead animal and vegetable substances may have more important effects, as when suspended fecal matter produces irritation of the whole alimentary tract. On the other hand, living things, such as the ova of entozoa, the nematoid worms and small leeches may give rise at once to certain grave disorders, or algæ may act on sulphates and disengage sulphuretted hydrogen."

Pure water is one of God's best gifts to man, and if that is allowed to be adulterated the impairment of our health and the destruction of our happiness is sure to follow.

In the samples of dug well waters which have recently been analyzed, the following animalculæ in addition to those given above were found by the use of the different powers of the microscope:

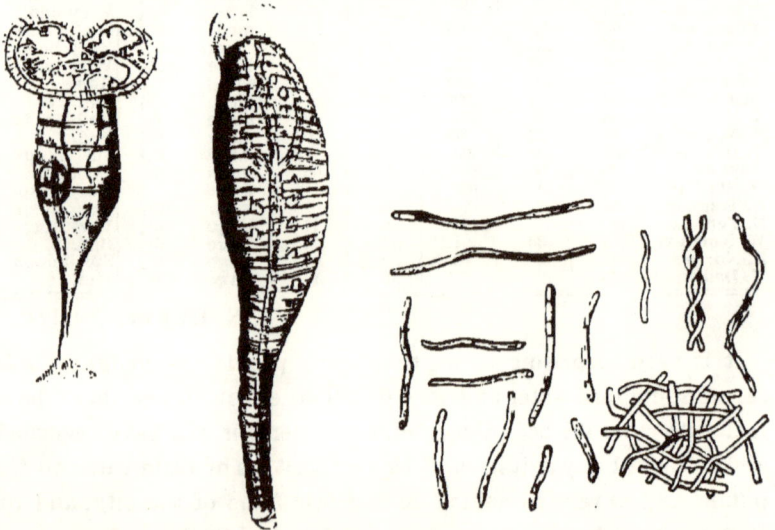

Megalotrocha flavicans.   Glossiphonia bioculata.   Vibrio.

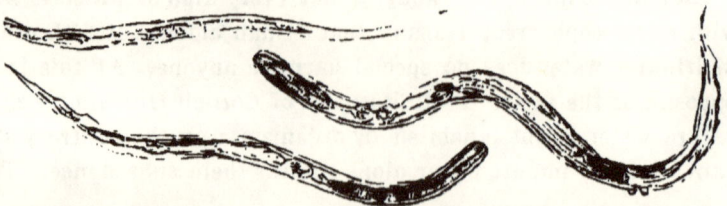

Anguillula fluviatilis.   Anguillula.
Anguillula aceti.

Vorticellina.

Bacteria.

Rotifera vulgaris.

Ophrydium versatile.

Halteria grandinella.

Cyclops quadricornis.

Alona quadrangularis.
Pluroxus trigonellus.

Stentor coerulleus.

Cypris tristriata.

Candona reptans.

Cythere inopinator.

At Indianapolis we have on the Board of Health three earnest and capable physicians who thoroughly understand the present necessities and stand ready to enforce all laws pertaining to public health ; but our laws on hygiene are very inefficient, and the power and usefulness of the board are unwisely limited ; therefore the board can do little towards averting the calamity already upon us. The Board of Health need more money, more men and the largest liberty of action.

We shall never have a healthy city until the health department is advanced to the position it deserves. We need a vigorous public sentiment in favor of cleanliness and hygienic measures. The best thought and energies of physicians and scientists everywhere should be directed to questions pertaining to water supply, sewerage and garbage of cities, and if necessary to secure proper legislation, the people must arise in their might and compel timid and shortsighted rulers to give better laws on sanitary matters and more money to make the laws effective.